Quiet Thoughts For The Quiet Hour

PATIENCE STRONG

Silently

Silently the seed swells in the earth—and the unborn
child awaits its birth ... Silently the snow falls, feather-
light. Silently the stars dance through the night ...
Silently as in a lovely dream—glides the swan upon the
moving stream. Silently roots spread and buds unclose.
Silently dawn comes and sunset glows.

Silently the mystic meditates. Silently he watches and he waits. Silently the grail of truth is sought—in the quiet sanctuary of thought ... Man creates the world's cacophony—by speech and motion. God works silently.

When Troubles Come

When troubles come we find our truest
friends. The knowledge of their loyal
affection lends—a glow to gloom, a
cheering, warming ray—that helps us face
the darkness of the day.

The word that heartens and the
kindly thought—give us courage, comfort
and support ... If we have proved a friend
to somebody—we too find friendship in
adversity.

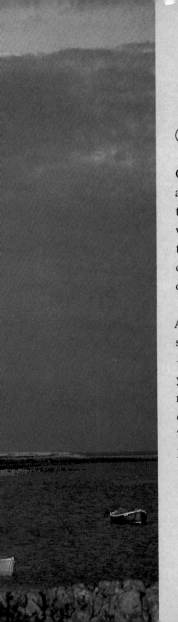

Beautiful Cloud

Over my head there's a threatening cloud,
a cloud with a menacing look—heavy and
thick like a layer of smoke as black as the
wing of a rook—spread like a canopy over
the roofs. Beneath it the garden goes grey—
chilling the flesh as the deep shadow falls,
quenching the light of the day.

An island of gloom in the blue of the
sky. Unmoving it seems at first sight
—like some great trouble that darkens
your life and changes your world overnight ... Beautiful cloud. Yes, a beautiful
cloud, although it is sombre and cold—
There's glory behind it, for now
I can see—its edging of luminous gold.

The Instrument

Play life like an instrument, making melodies.
Change the daily discords into harmonies ...
Draw the sweetness from it. Somebody may hear
—the tune behind the strident sounds that jar
upon the ear. Make your music as you move
through the world's distress—Someone passing
by may catch your note of happiness ... Play
life gently play it softly. Play with style and
grace—bringing beauty out of what is dull and
commonplace.

Use Your Eyes

If you're bored with life—just use your
eyes. Look at all those stars up in the
skies. Take a walk along some country
lane. Use your eyes a bit and think again.

Go and study Nature's book of
words. Watch the ducks, the sheep, the
fish, the birds—and the insects darting
to and fro. It's a great and fascinating
show.

Get out of yourself and you will
see—something that will cure your
malady ... A world of wonder all around
you lies. Look out of your window.
Use your eyes.

Reminders

Cast your eye across the country looking north, south,
east or west—and the symbol of our faith in flint or
brick or stone expressed—You will see on towers and

steeples pointing to the sky above—the uplifted cross of
Christ, a silent witness to the Love—that enfolds the
towns and hamlets where the parish churches stand—
Mute reminders of the God who holds the whole
world in His hands.

I Walked in Memory Lane Today

I walked in Memory Lane today. It was roses all the way—until I heard a voice that said—Turn back. Walk not the path ahead.

But on I pressed till suddenly — thorns and nettles tortured me ... My fingers bled, my sleeve was rent—as down the tangled track I went.

Go not too often or too far — along the road where memories are—but find content and pleasures new in what the present holds for you.

The Whisperers

I thought that snow had fallen overnight—when
I saw the willow ringed with white—like a necklace
looped around the tree. Mystified, I crossed
the lawn to see—snowdrops. Yes, the
snowdrops back again—bright with beaded
drops of frozen rain.

Every year it happens. Every year — And
yet when first I look and see them here—they
always seem to take me by surprise—when
winter's pall hangs heavy from the skies ... Too
soon, I say. But as I stoop to stare—at the little
flowerlets swinging there—I catch the whispered
message that they bring—and hail them as the
harbingers of Spring.

One by One

You do not have to take in one great stride—
the busy day that lies ahead of you. When
troubles loom around on every side — and
nowhere can you see a clear way through—
Just take it step by step and you will find—
fears fade like snowflakes melting in the sun ...
The worst things happen only in the mind—
and problems are disposed of one by one.

A New Lease of Life

A new lease of life is granted to the trees
at winter's going. See in garden, park and
lane the fresh new sap is flowing. This
the law in Nature's kingdom; leases are
renewed. Year by year without a break
the bare boughs are endued—with the
power of strength restored from root to
tip again—thrilling with vitality in fibre,
leaf and vein.

A new lease of life we too desire
when youth has lost its rapture. April
beauty and its bloom in vain we would
capture—but unlike the stricken branch
that spring's light touch revives—Time
in control and measures out our little
lives ... Only in the country of the mind
can we enjoy—the happiness perennial
that nothing can destroy.

The Light Comes Back

The beautiful light comes back again—feeble
and faint at the windowpane ... Visible now
are the casement bars—framing the slowly
fading stars.

Deep is the hush on the night's last edge—
as the first bird in some hidden hedge—
quickens the garden with one sweet note—out
of its quivering tiny throat.

And at his calling the world awakes. The
light comes back and the silence breaks ... Rise,
bow your head and for mercy pray. God is
sending another day.

Time Steps Out

Time is slow when we are young, but as the
years proceed—Time steps out and seems to
move at twice its former speed ... Swiftly are
the milestones passed—we see them flashing by
—Quickly do the birthdays come—Time races
... seasons fly.

Do not bank upon the future — It's not
yours to plan—No one but your Maker knows
the measure of your span ... We should always
live each day as if it were the last—the only
chance to make amends for failings of the past.

The Calvary Cross

What is the meaning of the cross? The cross
means sacrifice; submission to authority—the
paying of the price—demanded for the ransom
of the world, its soul to win—Nothing less
could make propitiation for its sin.

This is the sign of Calvary, the living,
saving sign. Defeat become a victory. And now
through bread and wine—we eat and drink the
sacraments as a memorial—of Friday's bitter
agony and Sunday's miracle.

This the redemptive festival. The centuries
have passed—but still we hail our risen King and
to this faith hold fast ... Let the wonder of its
meaning seep into the mind. Easter means
salvation and new life for all mankind.

So Little

The gentle smile, the reconciling touch—can
cost so little and can mean so much—to heal a
breach or mend a friendship broken—a letter
written, or a sentence spoken.

What hurts and pangs we suffer needlessly!
What pains inflict, because we cannot see—how
much we lose through conflicts and contentions
—poisoning life with quarrels and dissensions.

Let them all go and love triumphant be —
over all evil, hate, greed, jealousy ... Love's
tender word, forbearing and forgiving—brings
to the heart true peace and joy of living.

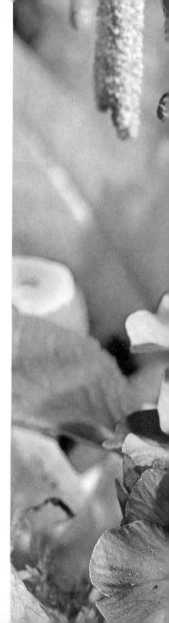

Specially for You

When you watch the lilac tassels swinging
in the breeze—catch the lilting rhapsodies
of songbirds in the trees—and see around
you everywhere the fresh life breaking
through—Take it as a gift from heaven,
specially for you.

Though you don't deserve it — it's
for you, this carnival. Pass not by with
blinkered eye. This is a miracle—of resur-
rection and revival. Feel it in your heart.
It is something personal, so do not draw
apart—missing what is wonderful and
beautiful and true—the festival you
somehow feel is specially for you. It's as
if God knew your need and sent for your
delight—this lovely April symphony of
fragrance, sound and sight.

Let There be Lights

The moon is playing hide and seek. It dips and swings
from peak to peak: a little silver coracle—becalmed,
and then invisible—plunged into an inky cloud—but
suddenly serene and proud—poised upon a wave's
bright crest. How could I sleep? How can I rest—
when there beyond my windowpane—through fitful
storms of driving rain—I watch the fascinating play—
of glitter, gloom and starry spray.

No magic television screen — could capture such a
lovely scene. And all I have to do is lie—and see this
drama of the sky ... Thus it has sailed, that fairy
barque—through immeasurable dark—since God first
said, Let there be lights: sun for the days and moon
for the nights.